depression and mood disorders

Judith Levin

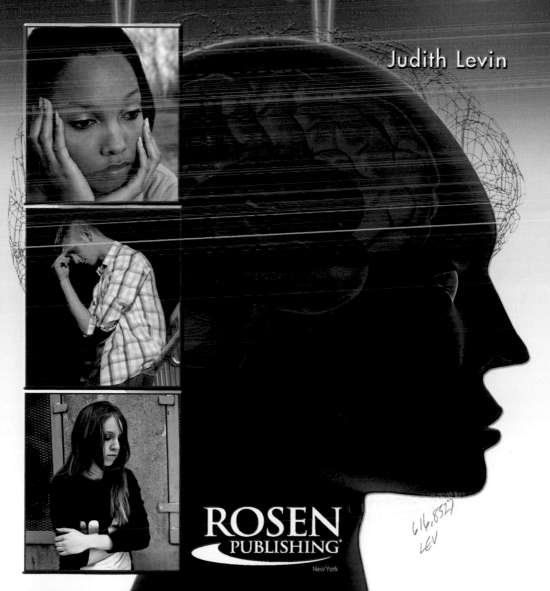

ROSEN
PUBLISHING®

New York

Published in 2009 by The Rosen Publishing Group, Inc.
29 East 21st Street, New York, NY 10010

Library of Congress Cataloging-in-Publication Data

Levin, Judith (Judith N.), 1956–
Depression and mood disorders / Judith Levin.—1st ed.
    p.cm.—(Teen mental health)
ISBN-13: 978-1-4042-1798-0 (library binding)
1. Depression, Mental—Juvenile literature. I. Title.
RC537.L478 2009
616.85'27—dc22

                                                                    2008000554

Manufactured in the United States of America

contents

chapter one

What Is Depression?

We all get the blues sometimes. But when those bad feelings hang on for weeks or months, it's probably more than a response to the ordinary hard times that everyone goes through in life. It may be an illness called depression.

If you're depressed you probably feel sad, discouraged, and hopeless for an extended time. You may have trouble functioning. You might feel exhausted all the time and have difficulty thinking clearly or quickly.

Sometimes, it's hard to tell the difference between general sadness and actual depression. They are not necessarily one and the same.

Sometimes, you might not even feel sad. Instead, you feel flat and "blah" and unable to care about anything. Recent studies show that more than 20 percent of teens have emotional problems. One-third of adolescents attending psychiatric clinics suffer from depression. Depression affects 20 percent of all adult women, 10 percent of all adult men, and 5 percent of all adolescents worldwide. It is the most common psychological problem in the United States. And it's a dangerous problem. "Depression is a disorder most commonly associated with adolescent suicide," says Dr. W. Michael Nelson, professor of psychiatry at Xavier University in Cincinnati, Ohio.

Unfortunately, most depressed teens never get the professional help they need. Some people believe that only "crazy" people seek the help of a mental health expert. But that's not true. Serious depression isn't something that you can simply "get over" or break out of. There is nothing wrong with seeking professional help, just as you would if you got a really bad flu.

Ten
Great Questions
to Ask Your
Therapist

1. What will happen in therapy?

2. Will my therapist tell my parents or my school what I say?

3. Can I call my therapist between sessions?

4. If I need an antidepressant, how long will it be before it starts to work?

5. If I have side effects from the antidepressants, what should I do? Are there any possible side effects that mean I should call the doctor right away?

6. Does having depression mean I'm crazy?

7. What can I do to help with my own treatment?

8. When someone I love is depressed, how can I help?

9. How can I talk to other teens who share my feelings?

10. What should I do if I'm feeling suicidal?

If you can't seem to shake the blues—or if you know someone who can't—you do not have to feel hopeless or alone. Depression can be treated and, in most cases, relieved.

It Can Happen to Anyone

It's a common belief that people with depression cannot function, but many depressed individuals can actually keep going to work or school. Some take medication or get some other form of treatment. Many try to carry on in spite of their deep, emotional pain. Famous people who have struggled with depression include U.S. president Abraham Lincoln, journalist Mike Wallace, comedian Rodney Dangerfield, poet Sylvia Plath, statesman Winston Churchill, artist Georgia O'Keefe, singers Janet Jackson and A. J. McLean, musicians Kurt Cobain and Gerard Way, and writers Virginia Woolf, Ernest Hemingway, and Mark Twain.

Some people are able to carry on with their lives despite major

Anyone can be struck by depression. Abraham Lincoln, considered by many to be America's greatest president, suffered from crippling bouts of the ailment.

7

depressive episodes. Others are knocked flat by less major ones. Perhaps this shouldn't be surprising. Some people carry on with their lives when they are very ill—undergoing treatment for cancer, for instance—and others take to their beds at the first sign of a cold. Individuals respond differently to depression, just as they do to other life experiences. Depression is only one part of who a person is.

Depression Statistics

Depression is remarkably common. Most studies show that at any given time, about one in eight American teens has depression. Overall, anywhere from 5 to 15 percent of the U.S. adult population will suffer from depression at some time. Another 5 percent experience mild symptoms or feel blue. At least one person in four has a serious depressive episode during his or her lifetime.

Experts say 70 percent of people treated for depression will experience the illness again. One out of every three people who have suffered from depression never has another serious problem with it. In a nutshell: Lots of people experience depression, lots of people get over it, and some people may get it again if they've had it before.

Symptoms of Depression

People who are depressed may feel sad all the time. But depression can affect people differently. It can affect you physically. For example, depression can make you feel tired, and yet you may have trouble sleeping at night. (Or, you might sleep excessively.) You might lose your appetite,

Symptoms of depression often involve a lack of motivation, as well as antisocial behavior, loss of appetite, and excessive sleeping.

or you may suddenly start overeating. You may have strange aches and pains and wonder if you are getting sick.

Depression also has emotional and mental symptoms. When you're depressed, nothing seems to work out the way you'd hoped. Whatever you do seems to go wrong. Even if it doesn't, you can see only the bad things. After several failures, you begin to think nothing will ever work out. "See—why did I even bother trying?" you might ask yourself. "I knew I was going to mess things up." A depressed person can feel hopeless, helpless, worthless, and, worst of all, alone. It becomes easy for depressed people to feel trapped by their troubles and become withdrawn.

Types of Depression

Many of the symptoms of mild depression are the same as those of major depression. The difference lies in how severe the symptoms are and how often the person experiences them.

If a person is grieving from loss or the death of a loved one, then sadness is a reaction that is to be expected. If the sadness persists, however, it may take professional judgment to decide if a person is still grieving or is becoming depressed. Unfortunately, friends, relatives, and family doctors may miss the signs that point toward a need for professional help. In such cases, clinical depression (depression requiring treatment) sometimes goes undiagnosed and untreated.

People overlook depression because so many symptoms can hide it. If someone experiences headaches, back pain, irritable bowel syndrome, chronic fatigue, or sleep problems, symptoms of these physical ailments can mask depression. Anxiety, too, often accompanies depression. So, someone may experience feelings of panic, shortness of breath, and rapid heartbeat and not recognize the symptoms as being part of underlying depression. In addition, different types of depression present different symptoms that can affect a person to very different degrees. Types of depression are listed as follows:

Depression doesn't only affect the mind. Physical symptoms can appear in severe cases, since the mind and body are interdependent.

- **Reactive depression** is a temporary depression. It is related to feelings that arise because of a specific life situation. Symptoms can be severe, but they usually subside within two weeks to six months.

- **Major depression** is a serious condition that can cause someone to be unable to function and possibly attempt suicide. Major depression can go in cycles, meaning someone who has it might get over it (sometimes even without treatment), but then it comes back. Treating major depression can make it go away faster and make it less likely to come back.

- **Dysthymia** describes a chronically depressed mood. That means the symptoms are less intense than with major depression, but the depression lasts longer. A major depression will be diagnosed if the person has had severe symptoms for two weeks; dysthymia is diagnosed only after two years of illness. (That doesn't mean the person should wait two years to seek help!)

- **Bipolar disorder** (also called manic-depressive disorder) involves major depressive episodes alternating with periods of extremely energetic activity. People who are manic may need very little sleep and be full of ideas, or they may go on wild shopping sprees. But then they crash into a depression. Bipolar disorder is the "roller coaster" of depressions. About 1 percent of the American population experiences bipolar disorder in a given year.

- **Atypical depression** is not constant. A person with this condition might seem deeply depressed for a few days, then be fine for a while, or anxious and cranky.
- **Seasonal affective disorder (SAD)** is often referred to as "winter blues." It is a psychological and physical reaction to lack of sunlight. Typically, people who have SAD experience the onset of depression in late autumn. This depression, which can be mild or major, then clears up in early spring, as daylight hours start to get longer. This condition becomes more common as distance from the equator increases. In Greenland, where winter nights go on round the clock, seasonal affective disorder is common.
- **Postpartum depression** results from the enormous hormonal changes that take place when women give birth and begin the challenges of caring for an infant. About two-thirds of new mothers experience this form of depression. However, for about 10 to 15 percent of mothers, postpartum depression develops into clinical depression.

chapter two

Causes of Depression

People have recognized depression for thousands of years. In the fifth century BCE, the Greek physician Hippocrates wrote about an illness he called melancholia. Melancholics, he wrote, suffered from "aversion to food, despondency, sleeplessness, irritability, restlessness." That means, they didn't feel like eating, couldn't sleep, and were cranky. Hippocrates believed melancholia was a disease of the body. He observed that some people seemed to be born more melancholic, some full of anger, some hopeful, and some calm. Melancholia might be inborn, he believed, or it might be set off by a traumatic or painful experience in a person's life. People who already tended to be melancholic by nature were especially vulnerable to these traumatic events. Hippocrates believed mostly in medicinal remedies. If you think about yourself and people you know, his way of looking at personalities makes sense. Some people, even little babies, do seem naturally happy and hopeful or naturally grouchy and ready to get mad.

The Greek philosopher Plato, on the other hand, emphasized how children's upbringing affected the people they became. Instead of seeing character as inborn, he was interested in how our families, neighborhoods, and schools shape us. Some later thinkers would decide melancholia was caused by the effects of the planet Saturn on the body, or by the influence of evil spirits. In any case, thousands of years ago, people had already raised (and disagreed about) the key question: Is depression a physical disease that can be cured by medicines? Or, is it a mental and spiritual

Greek physician Hippocrates wrote about depression millennia ago and studied the same question we ask today: Is the condition inborn or learned?

15

disorder that can be cured by looking at a person's background and changing the way he or she lives and thinks about life? This disagreement is still going on.

Depression is, after all, a mysterious disorder. Human life is full of problems and losses. Terrible things happen: natural disasters like floods, or human disasters like war. Family members die. People we love don't always love us back. Yet while some people weep, grieve, rage, and then are able to go on with their lives, others are just knocked flat by the same experiences. They may say, "I'm no good." They may say that it is not sadness they feel but deadness and numbness. In addition to having lost something outside themselves—a parent, a boyfriend, a house that burns down—they seem to have lost something inside themselves, too. To make this even more complicated, some people become depressed without suffering any obvious loss. In fact, it may be a great success that causes them to be depressed! No wonder people argue about the causes of depression and about how to help people who suffer from it.

The Psychology of Depression

Most experts believe depression develops from a combination of factors. Research shows that the biological children of someone with major depression are more likely to become depressed—even if they are adopted at birth and raised by people who are not depressed. So, that tells us that genetic inheritance plays a role.

Yet genes don't tell the whole story. If your mother or father suffers from depression, it may affect her or his ability to take care of you. You may have grown up feeling that you were a burden. As a small child, you may have felt that you did not deserve to be loved, or that it was your fault that your parent is distant or unhappy. (You may still feel this way.) These feelings may be reflected in your own depression.

Also, when you're a child, you learn from your parents how to respond to the world. If a parent responded to problems and challenges—a lost job or a power failure during a bad storm—by seeming helpless and full of despair, then you learn something very different than you would from a parent who meets challenges with energy and plans. One parent gives lessons in being afraid or giving up. The other shows that life's tough, but we're tougher! What you learn about yourself and the world around you becomes part of your brain chemistry.

Of course, babies are born with other characteristics besides a vulnerability to depression. Some newborns are easily soothed when they cry; others are easily startled and harder to comfort. These are not learned characteristics; they are inborn. If you observe little babies still in the hospital, you see that they are already different from one another.

It's also important to take into consideration other environmental factors. You were born into a family that will respond to your inborn traits in all sorts of ways. As a child, you may or may not have had a good "fit" with your family. For instance, a very calm child may be labeled "easy" and "good" to one family but sort of "out of it" to another. An extremely active, curious, and demanding child may seem "bad" to one family. The kid may grow up hearing, "Why can't you ever behave?" In another

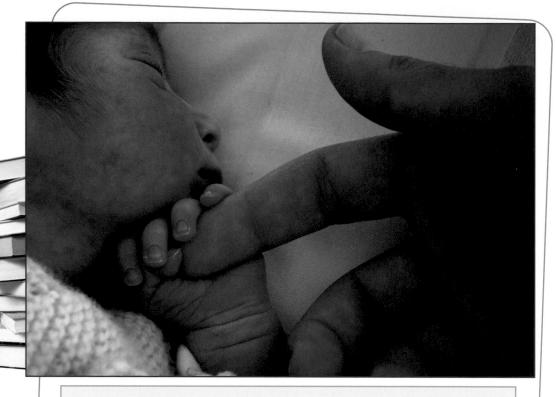

Doctors still know relatively little about depression, such as the question of whether we are born with the ailment or develop it later in life.

family, a parent might say of the same child, "Oh, well, that's just what I was like when I was that age" or, "What an energetic, interesting kid." The same parents may have an easier time raising one of their children than another. The child with a good "fit" in his or her family may have a more positive outlook and may find life's problems easier to bear.

As a newborn, you had all sorts of other inborn traits, including gender, skin color, ethnicity, and native intelligence. In addition, there are external factors such as economic class, geographical location, and regional climate. Timing matters, too, as you are born during a particular era in history. All of these things will affect the opportunities you have, the challenges you face, and the help that will be available to you as you grow. In some people, these factors will contribute to becoming depressed.

The Biology of Depression

In the 1920s, medical researchers identified chemicals called neurotransmitters. In more recent years, researchers have learned more about how these chemicals allow neurons (nerve cells) in the brain to communicate with one another. Neurons do not actually touch, so neuro-transmitters allow electrical impulses to leap the tiny gaps between cells. Just about all our thoughts, feelings, and experiences involve the neurotransmitters in our brains.

Researchers don't fully understand neurotransmitters, in part because these chemicals are hard to study. They are produced in tiny quantities and are hard to measure. In addition, the brain usually reabsorbs them, or takes them up, quickly.

Neurotransmitters are involved in regulating our moods and behaviors. For example, the hormone serotonin is a neurotransmitter that is particularly important to the way our brains communicate feelings of happiness. Researchers found that many depressed people have lower than normal levels of serotonin. So, they identified drugs that elevate the levels of serotonin, allowing the neurotransmitter to remain present in the brain longer than usual. In other words, the medications inhibit (slow down) the reuptake of serotonin. For this reason, these medications are called selective serotonin reuptake inhibitors, or SSRIs. Prozac, a depression medication you may have heard of, is an SSRI. Doctors don't yet know exactly how or why SSRIs work in treating depression, but often they do.

In other types of depression, the problem may be from too much of a neurotransmitter rather than too little. Melatonin, for example, is a hormone and neurotransmitter that regulates sleep patterns. Our bodies' production of melatonin increases on a nightly basis, while we sleep. And our melatonin levels are further elevated on a seasonal basis, during the short days and long nights of winter. In people suffering from seasonal affective disorder (SAD), melatonin levels are unusually high. So, in the case of SAD, drug therapy involves reducing the levels of melatonin or increasing it at more beneficial times during the day.

Yet depression as a disease is not simply a malfunction or lack of neurotransmitters the way diabetes, for instance, is a lack of the hormone insulin. In someone with type 1 diabetes, the pancreas has stopped making insulin. Without insulin, the human body cannot process blood sugar. However, when people with diabetes are given the right amounts of insulin, their bodies are almost always able to process blood sugar properly. But it is not easy to find the right amount of SSRIs to add, and they don't work immediately. What's worse is that SSRIs do not always work for people who are depressed. Perhaps most important, nobody knows why people begin to have a problem with their neurotransmitters in the first place.

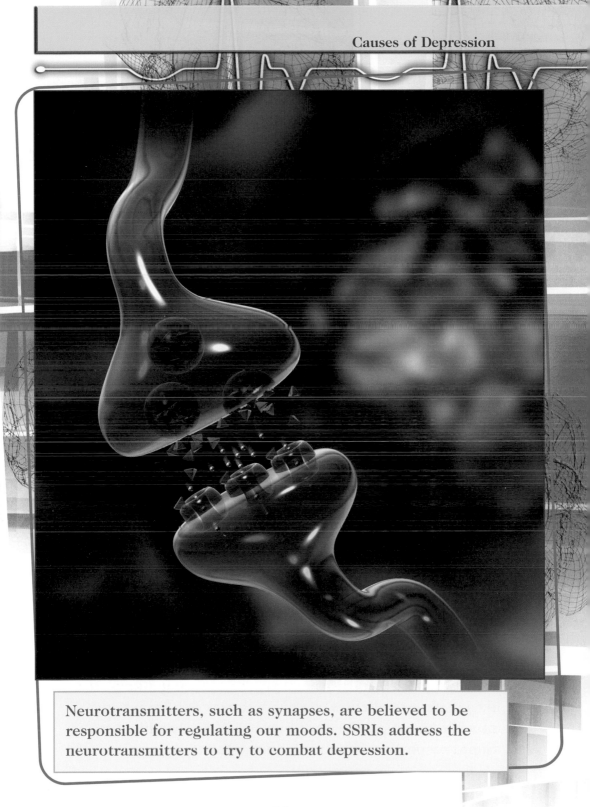

Neurotransmitters, such as synapses, are believed to be responsible for regulating our moods. SSRIs address the neurotransmitters to try to combat depression.

Other Changes in the Body

Researchers have found other physical changes in the bodies of people who are depressed. For example, many depressed people show elevated levels of cortisol in their blood. (Cortisol is an important hormone produced by the adrenal gland that helps the body respond to stress.) But many depressed people have normal levels of cortisol. So depression cannot be diagnosed by testing the blood for cortisol. There's some connection there, but no one knows what it is yet.

Additionally, there are diseases or disorders of other parts of the body that can cause depression. The thyroid gland is located in the front of your throat. It regulates metabolism, or the rate at which your cells convert fuel, or food, into energy. Hypothyroidism (an underactive thyroid condition) can cause dull hair, weight gain, and lack of energy. It may also cause depression. Yet if you have hypothyroidism, you need to take a pill that is a thyroid supplement, not an antidepressant.

There are two things to take away from this chemistry lesson. One is that since depression can be caused by something like hypothyroidism, a person who is depressed should always have a physical exam. The other is that while signs of depression may show up in our brain and body chemistry, we should not assume that depression is only caused by a problem in chemistry. Everything that happens to us affects the brain's chemistry. We do not yet know to what extent the brain's chemistry causes depression and to what extent people's experiences affect that chemistry. Some people may inherit a vulnerability to depression, as

Hypothyroidism is commonly associated with depression. One if its symptoms is lethargy, or an unnatural lack of energy.

they would inherit a vulnerability to heart disease. This means they are not born with depression, and they may not get it, but they are more likely to develop a depressive illness than someone born with a different biology.

Psychology Plus Biology Plus Society

So, there are many things that affect who you become. If part of what you become is depressed, then the causes of the depression will be some combination of things: the biology you're born with, plus all the experiences of your life and how they have shaped your brain.

Your brain continues to change throughout your life. In fact, the brain is able to change much more than researchers once thought. For example, some injury victims lose the use of crucial parts of their brains related to language. These people would not be expected to speak, but their brains often adapt, and other parts of the brain learn to perform language functions. This was previously thought to be impossible.

Sometimes, the cause of a depression is impossible to identify. Some serious depressions seem to come out of nowhere. But sometimes the cause may just not be obvious. Suppose you get a really big college scholarship. That might just make you happy—or it might have other meanings. Maybe it fulfills your parents' dreams but not your own. In addition, you may focus on the losses the scholarship brings with it, not the opportunities. If it means that you will be the first person in your family to go to college, you might feel you are deserting your family. Or, you might begin to feel that you will have to become someone different to succeed at college. You may, in your heart, wish to leave your family but feel guilty about that wish.

In the end, you might grapple successfully with all of the challenges the college scholarship will bring. But another teen in your situation might mystify friends, teachers, and family by becoming sad, guilty, sleepless, and overwhelmed.

chapter three

Teenage Depression

The teenage years are an emotional roller coaster, even if you're loved and well adjusted. For young people who are neglected or abused, being a teenager can be a nightmare.

Parents, teachers, friends, and relatives often find it difficult to recognize depression in a teenager. Instead of—or in addition to—symptoms such as a lack of interest and energy, withdrawal, hopelessness, and unusual sleep patterns, depressed teens tend to be intensely irritable, have angry outbursts, and show destructive

One of the physical symptoms of depression is a lack of appetite. Constantly skipping or refusing meals may be a sign of the condition.

behaviors such as alcohol or drug abuse. Eating disorders and cutting (self-mutilation) may also be symptoms of depression. But parents in particular may be entirely clueless about what's normal and what's not in their teenage child. Sometimes, you're not so sure yourself.

What Causes Teenage Depression?

The most common type of depression in teens is reactive depression. This is the type caused by some outside event or influence in your life.

Often, you have no control over the factors that cause reactive depression, which may involve:

- Death of a loved one
- Divorce of parents
- Conflicts or violence at home
- Physical illness
- Disability

- The end of a close friendship
- Challenges in school
- Pressure to succeed
- Peer pressure

Many teenagers work through their problems with the help of friends and family, and eventually, they feel better. Others, even those from loving and supportive homes, may need professional help to deal with their depression. It's nothing to be ashamed of.

What Makes Teenage Depression Different?

As a teen, you are in the midst of attempting to establish an identity independent of your family. You are also experiencing major hormonal changes, which can cause great emotional highs and severe lows, as well as extreme changes in sleep patterns. Any of these things can lead to deep emotional reactions. Other big teen stresses include identity issues, struggles among peer groups, and establishing sexual identity.

Teenagers who suffer from depression often act out instead of acting sad and withdrawn. Their behavior may be wild and angry, and they may not seem to care what happens to them or to anyone else. Getting into trouble at home, at school, or with the law may be their way of attracting attention to their problems. Adults don't always recognize teen depression. Instead, they see depressed teens as "bad" or "lazy," and they respond with anger or punishment.

During the teenage years, you are finding your identity by dressing and acting in your own way. This hard-fought struggle to develop your own style often brings about depression among your age group.

Symptoms of Teenage Depression

The adolescent years are a time of great change, both in mind and body. Teens are trying to become independent, and most will rebel against authority in some way. For that reason, the early signs of depression are often ignored. (Everyone knows teens are mouthy and have no manners, right?) So, it's easy for families and schools to miss the following behaviors as possible symptoms of depression:

- Long-term boredom
- "Acting out" (getting into trouble at home, at school, or with the law)
- Restlessness or agitation
- Cutting classes
- Considerable appetite or weight changes
- Drug or alcohol abuse
- Taking unnecessary risks
- Increased "accidents," some done on purpose to hurt oneself
- Sexual misconduct
- Poor performance in school, athletics, etc.
- Loss of friends; isolating themselves from others
- Headaches or other physical complaints
- Talk of suicide
- Ceasing to take showers and take care of physical appearance
- Developing a strong interest in art, poetry, movies, and music that focus on dark, sad, and violent images
- Hallucinations or unusual beliefs

Most adolescents go through periods of being bored with life, misbehaving, or taking risks. But when this kind of behavior goes too far or happens too often, it could be a sign of depression. Does this sound like you? Are you just doing stuff because everyone in your crowd does it? Or, does drinking or driving too fast ease some pain inside you? Do you like it if people think you're trouble? If this sounds like a friend, maybe have a talk, just the two of you. Let him or her know that you notice his or her behavior, and make it known you are concerned.

MYTHS AND FACTS

Myth: All people who are depressed look sad and cry a lot.

Fact: Sadness is a common symptom of depression, but it is not the only one. Even if people are sad, they may hide it. Someone who is depressed may seem angry— especially teenagers—or emotionless and withdrawn.

Myth: Asking people if they are thinking about suicide will plant the idea in their heads and make them more likely to try it.

Fact: Asking depressed people about suicide gives them a chance to say what's on their minds and increases the chances of their getting help. Asking about suicidal thoughts may actually prevent a suicide.

Myth: Depression only happens to people after something bad has happened to them.

Fact: Sometimes, depression seems to start for no reason at all, while someone's life is fine. Sometimes, it even starts when something good happens.

Myth: You should be able to snap out of your depression if you try hard enough.

Fact: People who are depressed usually need professional help. Believing that they could stop being depressed if they tried can become one more thing for a depressed person to feel guilty about.

Myth: Talking to a therapist is just whining and complaining, and it doesn't help.

Fact: Research shows that talking therapies can actually change the chemistry of the brain, just as medications do. They can also help people work out problems and avoid future depressions.

chapter four

Getting Help

Depression is treatable, but relatively few people get help when they need it. Among depressed adults, only one in three is treated. About 80 percent of people with depression can improve their mental health with psychotherapy (talking therapies), medication, or both.

Unfortunately, many people continue to believe that treatments do not work. Depression can make people feel totally hopeless, so it's hard for them to imagine that anyone or anything could make them feel better. That's where others can help.

Treatments

Depending on the individual patient, depression can be treated with various kinds of talking therapies, with medication, or with a combination of talking therapies and medication. And if these treatments do not work, there are some additional alternative treatments that may be used.

For a special type of depression called seasonal affective disorder (SAD), a patient may be treated by exposure to light. The person suffering from SAD may sit in front of a special lamp, ten to twenty times as bright as an ordinary lamp, for thirty or more minutes each day. This light therapy adjusts the way the body processes melatonin, leading to a lessening of the symptoms.

Light therapy is believed to help alleviate seasonal affective disorder by triggering certain chemicals in the brain that make people happy.

What Therapy Can Do

Depression is an illness that may require long-term care. Verbal therapy occurs over several sessions (meetings) for a period of months or years. These sessions are usually helpful for several reasons. Some depression occurs when a person is trying to avoid dealing with a painful memory or unresolved problems. In these cases, the therapist will focus on the past. Therapists also look at the present. A therapist may be able to help you identify things going on now in your life that trigger depression. He or she may help you develop ways to cope with problems at school or at home. A therapist's job is to listen to you, never to judge you, and to help you find solutions to problems or confusions. More than anyone else in your life, a therapist is supposed to have only your best interests in mind. Friends and family want you to think about their needs, too. That's fair. But a therapist is there for the sole purpose of helping you.

If you are a minor, you are probably not old enough to legally consent (agree) to treatment, and a parent or guardian must consent for you. If this is the case, your parents or guardian are within their legal rights to ask your therapist about what you say in therapy. Your therapist should be honest with you regarding the level of privacy you can expect. Good therapy relies on a trusting relationship between the patient and the therapist, so most therapists try hard to maintain your privacy when it comes to the content of your therapy.

If you have reached a certain age (eighteen in most U.S. states), your therapist cannot tell your parents—or anyone else—what you say in therapy. However, being old enough for patient/therapist confidentiality does not mean that what you say in therapy is 100 percent confidential. If your therapist believes you are in immediate danger of hurting yourself or someone else, he or she has the legal responsibility to disclose your information to protect your life or the life of someone else.

Choosing the Right Therapist

You need to be able to trust your therapist; that's the most important thing. Beyond that, however, you have a lot of options when it comes to therapy. Different types of professional therapists serve patients with different needs.

Psychologists are mental health professionals who have gone through many years of training but are not licensed medical doctors. They cannot prescribe drugs. Teens typically work with psychologists who specialize in treating adolescents.

Social workers are trained professionals who work with groups and families, as well as individuals. Social workers typically have a master's degree and deal with a wide range of issues and populations.

Psychiatrists are licensed doctors who have completed medical school. They can prescribe medications.

There are other licensed or certified psychotherapists whose titles vary. For example, in some states, you will find licensed professional counselors (LPCs), certified addiction counselors (CACs), or licensed marriage and family therapists (LMFTs).

Good therapists are truthful about what will happen during therapy. They talk with you about the kind of therapy they will do, how the sessions will be run, and what to expect. Different therapists will have different approaches to your situation, based on their training.

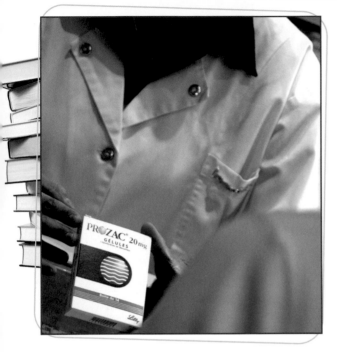

Sometimes, medication is the only apparent solution to treat depression. Based on your psychological evaluation, your doctor may prescribe specific drugs to treat your individual condition.

Drug Treatment: Antidepressants

Sometimes, therapists are unable to assign a cause to your depression, and your depression does not respond to other types of therapy. In this case, a psychiatrist or other doctor may decide to prescribe one or more antidepressant drugs. If someone is severely depressed, then medications may be prescribed even before verbal therapy begins. Your psychiatrist may also be your therapist; or your psychiatrist may prescribe and supervise your medications while you are in therapy with someone else. Doctors prescribe several types of antidepressant drugs to treat different aspects of depression.

Other Therapies

If you have been diagnosed with depression, then you should consider therapy and/or antidepressants your main treatments. But, while you are in treatment and when you have gotten over depression, there are things that may help you feel better. They may help in your treatment or prevent a relapse. Medications are not the only way to affect brain chemistry. Things you choose to do and how you choose to spend your time also affect it.

Extensive research points to the importance of exercise, particularly exercise that raises your heart rate and makes you breathe deeper and faster. This type of exercise, called aerobic exercise, is known to elevate mood, relieve anxiety, and improve appetite, sleep, and self-esteem. Studies show that aerobic exercise actually changes your brain chemistry for a while and releases endorphins (natural chemicals that make you feel good) into your bloodstream. Dance, ride a bike, dig a garden, or go running.

One of the most proven treatments for depression is an active, outgoing lifestyle that includes socializing and physical activity.

Alternative Treatments

The United Nations World Health Organization recognizes acupuncture as an effective treatment for moderate depression. This involves having a specially trained person insert very thin needles into your skin. No one really knows why it sometimes works, but that's true of some more conventional kinds of medicine, too. Other alternative treatments that are known to work include massage therapy, music and art therapy, yoga, and sitting meditation.

Making Therapy Work

Doctors and therapists can't magically "cure" someone with depression. They can only help depressed people get better. Patients must decide for themselves that they want to improve. Depressed persons must believe that recovery is possible, yet they must also face up to the facts that there are no guarantees and that effective treatment is different for everyone.

Therapy works best when the whole family gets involved. Therapy can help a person change certain behaviors or ways of thinking, but the depressed individual may not be the only one who needs to change. Other family members and close friends must look at their own behavior, too.

If you begin drug therapy, the drugs must be taken as prescribed. It is important not to stop taking an anti-depressant once you feel better. Many people have made this poor decision. You're feeling better because of the medication, even though it doesn't seem that way. In time, your doctor may say you can go off the medicine, but you may have to stay on your drug treatment for an extended time.

Opening up and expressing your feelings to loved ones is a great first step on the road to treating depression and mood disorders.

Depression Is a Treatable Illness

With the right therapy, as many as eight out of ten people can recover from their depression. More than half of these will at least begin to feel better within a month to six weeks. But sometimes it takes longer, and the waiting is hard.

Depression takes away a person's energy and hope. The world seems darker, and it is hard to believe that life ever seemed good or could seem good again. Feeling better takes time, patience, and work. When you are depressed, you cannot simply will yourself to get better. But you can do things that will help you recover and perhaps prevent a recurrence of the depression.

Ask for help. Demand help if necessary. Take the medication that has been prescribed for you. Find a therapist you trust, and work hard to help that person help you. Tell him or her the truth, even if the truth is ugly and there is no one else you can tell. Get exercise and eat well, even though you don't want to.

Try to remember that your darkest and most negative thoughts may not be the truth, even though they seem like the truth. Don't focus on these thoughts, as they are more likely the voice of your depression. Instead, try to focus on the voices of people who say they love you and want to help.

antidepressants Drugs prescribed by a doctor to treat depression.

anxiety Extreme state of nervousness or fear.

bipolar disorder A form of mental illness in which a person's mood swings from intense sadness to high excitability; also called manic depression.

counselor Person who offers advice and help with special problems.

depression Mental illness in which sadness and gloom overwhelm a person's daily life.

gene Part of a body cell that carries traits from parents to children.

hormones Chemicals in the body that help it to grow, stay healthy, or respond to stress.

mania State of high, unnatural excitement or enthusiasm.

neurotransmitter Chemical that transmits messages from one cell to the next.

psychiatrist A medical doctor who treats mental illness.

psychologist A person who has studied human behavior and treats problems of the mind.

psychotherapy Therapy based on examining your own personality, emotions, and subconscious mind.

suicide The intentional killing of oneself.

symptom Sign or indication of an illness.

synapse The space through which a nervous impulse passes from one neuron (nerve cell) to another.

therapist A person trained to help patients recover from illness or injury.

therapy Treatment for a disease or condition.

American Association of Suicidology
4201 Connecticut Avenue NW, Suite 408
Washington, DC 20008
(202) 237-2280
Web site: http://www.suicidology.org
This national organization seeks to educate and train suicide prevention professionals to end the occurrence of suicide.

American Foundation for Suicide Prevention
120 Wall Street, 22nd Floor
New York, NY 10005
(888) 333-AFSP (2377)
Web site: http://www.afsp.org
This national nonprofit organization provides research and outreach
for people who may be at risk for suicide.

American Psychiatric Association
1000 Wilson Boulevard, Suite 1825
Arlington, VA 22209-3901
(703) 907-7300
Web site: http://www.psych.org
The American Psychiatric Association is an organization of psychiatrists
who work together to ensure humane care and effective treatment
for people with mental disorders.

Child and Adolescent Bipolar Foundation (CABF)
1000 Skokie Boulevard, Suite 425
Wilmette, IL 60091
(847) 256-8525
Web site: http://www.bpkids.org

CABF is a nonprofit, parent-led, Web-based membership organization of families raising children and teens diagnosed with, or at risk for, bipolar disorder.

Depression and Bipolar Support Alliance (DBSA)
730 North Franklin Street, Suite 501
Chicago, IL 60610-7204
(800) 826-3632
Web site: http://www.dbsalliance.org
The DBSA educates and helps those suffering from mood disorders.

International Foundation for Research and
        Education on Depression (iFred)
7040 Bembe Beach Road, Suite 100
Annapolis, MD 21403
(410) 268-0044
Web site: http://www.ifred.org
iFred is dedicated to researching causes of depression, supporting those dealing with the disease, and combating the stigma associated with it.

National Alliance on Mental Illness (NAMI)
2107 Wilson Boulevard, Suite 300
Arlington, VA 22201-3042
(800) 950-NAMI (6264)
Web site: http://www.nami.org
NAMI is the nation's largest grassroots mental health organization dedicated to improving the lives of persons living with serious mental illness.

National Foundation for Depressive Illness, Inc.
P.O. Box 2257
New York, NY 10116
(800) 248-4344
Web site: http://www.depression.org
This is a good resource for information on depression. Its Web site offers links to major associations dealing with depression.

National Institute of Mental Health (NIMH)
6001 Executive Boulevard, Room 8184
MSC 9663
Bethesda, MD 20892-9663
(866) 615-6464 or (301) 443-4513
Web site: http://www.nimh.nih.gov
NIMH is a component of the National Institutes of Health (NIH), the federal government's principal biomedical and behavioral research agency and part of the U.S. Department of Health and Human Services.

National Mental Health Association (NMHA)
2000 North Beauregard Street, 6th Floor
Alexandria, VA 22311
(703) 684-7722
Web site: http://www.nmha.org
The NMHA is the country's oldest and largest nonprofit organization addressing all aspects of mental health and mental illness.

Suicide Awareness Voices of Education (SAVE)
9001 East Bloomington Freeway, Suite 150
Bloomington, MN 55420
(952) 946-7998

Web site: http://www.save.org
This nonprofit group mainly comprises survivors of suicide.

Web Sites

Due to the changing nature of Internet links, Rosen Publishing has developed an online list of Web sites related to the subject of this book. This site is updated regularly. Please use this link to access the list:

http://www.rosenlinks.com/tmh/damd

Cobain, Bev. *When Nothing Matters Anymore: A Survival Guide for Depressed Teens*. Minneapolis, MN: Free Spirit Publishing, 1998.

Crook, Marion. *Out of Darkness: Teens Talk About Suicide*. Vancouver, BC: Arsenal Pulp Press, 2004.

Gelman, Amy. *Coping with Depression and Other Mood Disorders*. New York, NY: The Rosen Publishing Group, Inc., 2000.

Marchetta, Melina. *Saving Francesca*. New York, NY: Knopf, 2004.

Martin, Michael. *Teen Depression*. Farmington Hills, MI: Lucent, 2004.

Roleff, Tamara, ed. *Teen Suicide*. San Diego, CA: Greenhaven Press, 2000.

Winkler, Kathleen. *Teens, Depression, and the Blues: A Hot Issue*. Berkeley Heights, NJ: Enslow, 2000.

Wolpert, Lewis. *Malignant Sadness: The Anatomy of Depression*. New York, NY: Free Press, 2000.

Vizzini, Ned. *It's Kind of a Funny Story*. New York, NY: Miramax, 2006.

Zucker, Faye, and Joan E. Huebl. *Beating Depression: Teens Find Light at the End of the Tunnel*. New York, NY: Franklin Watts, 2006.

About the Author

Judith N. Levin is an author and librarian with a variety of nonfiction books to her credit, most of which were written on diverse subjects including history, science, technology, and health.

Photo Credits

Cover, p. 1 (top left) © www.istockphoto.com/Sheryl Griffin; cover, p. 1 (middle left) © www.istockphoto.com/Joshua Blake; cover, p. 1 (bottom left) © www.istockphoto.com/Juan Estey; cover (right) © www.istockphoto.com/Nicholas Monu; cover, pp. 1, 3 (head and brain) © www.istockphoto.com/Vasiliy Yakobchuk; p. 3 (laptop) www.istockphoto.com/Brendon De Suza; p. 3 and additional page backgrounds (books) © www.istockphoto.com/Michal Koziarski; pp. 4, 14, 25, 32 (head) © www.istockphoto.com; p. 4 © www.istockphoto.com/Nicholas Monu; p. 5 © www.istockphoto.com/ericsphotography; p. 7 Hulton/Archive/Getty Images; p. 9 © www.istockphoto.com/Joseph Hoyle; p. 11 © www.istockphoto.com/Roberta Osborne; p. 14 © www.istockphoto.com/Jason Lugo; p. 15 © Roger-Viollet/The Image Works; p. 18 © www.istockphoto.com/Serdar Yagci; p. 21 © Gary Carlson/Photo Researchers, Inc.; p. 23 Jason Hetherington/Stone/Getty Images; p. 25 © www.istockphoto.com/Quavondo Nguyen; p. 26 © David Kelly Crow/PhotoEdit; p. 28 © Lauren Greenfield/VII/AP Images; p. 32 © www.istockphoto.com/Tracy Whiteside; p. 33 © Science Museum/SSPL/The Image Works; p. 36 © AJPhoto/Photo Researchers, Inc.; p. 37 © www.istockphoto.com/Dennis Babenko; p. 39 © www.istockphoto.com/Nancy Louie.

Designer: Nelson Sá; Editor: Nicholas Croce
Photo Researcher: Cindy Reiman